STATO PONTIFICIO ROMANO

The Anglican Patriarchate of Rome (Stato Pontificio, Anglican Rite Roman Catholic Church) is an ecclesiastical sovereignty by right of Rome with an independent government in special consultative status with the United Nations Economic and Social Council. Additionally, we descend from the See of Utrecht, which was granted autonomy in 1145 by Pope Eugene III and confirmed in 1520 by Pope Saint Leo X in the Bull Debitum Pastoralis, this right becoming known as the Leonine Privilege. As the sole successor of Pope Saint Leo X and temporal successor of St. Peter the Apostle in Italy and Britain, the Patriarchate is fully Catholic and holds the same canonical authority as the Roman Communion (Vatican). The Patriarchate is the ecclesiastical successor to temporal Rome, the temporal patrimony of the Roman Empire claimed historically by right of the papacy. The succession passed to the Patriarchate after Benedict XVI by right of Rome and Florence, with the Papa-Prince of Rome with papal authority as temporal successor of St. Peter, and the Pope-Bishop of Rome as spiritual successor of St. Peter and de facto sovereign of the Vatican City-State. Although administratively independent, the Apostolic See of the Patriarchate embraces as brethren other Catholic and Anglican bodies, such as the current Roman Communion (commonly referred to as the Roman Catholic Church), the Anglican Ordinariate, and the Anglican Communion. The Imperial Roman Church is defined as the Anglican Patriarchate and the churches of all Bishops recognised by the Apostolic See.

PONTIFICAL FLORENTINE-ROMAN HOUSE OF JOHNSON-IVREA-ITALIA-BARCELONA

By
Gr.D. Daniel Coberly v. Reichenberg, Prince v. Würzburg

STATO PONTIFICIO
2022

H.H.E. Papa Rutherford I,
Prince of the Romans & Grand Duke of Ruthenia

and

H.I.R.M. Grand Duchess Hanna Aliaksandrauna,
Princess of the Romans & Grand Duchess of Ruthenia

Pontifical Florentine-Roman House of Johnson-Ivrea-Italia-Barcelona

The Pont. Flor.-Rom. House of Johnson-Ivrea-Italia-Barcelona is the ecclesiastical successor and heir in Imperial Italy to the Burgundian House of Arles and the Spanish Houses of Ivrea and Barcelona and is the ecclesiastical successor to the Roman Empire. Of ancient origin, the house descends from the Roman Empire, Byzantine Empire, Holy Roman Empire, Spanish Empire, Imperial Kingdom of Italy, the Merovingian Dynasty, the French Capetian Dynasty, the Normans in Britain, the Rurikid Dynasty of Kievan Rus, and the dynasties of Poland, Hungary, Bohemia, and Bulgaria, among others. Spanning the centuries, the family's ancestors were found in Europe from west to east. They left their mark on history wherever they went.

In the 17th century, direct lines of the present household came to the New World colonies of Britain, the Netherlands, and France. There they were of the nobility and positions of prominence in the military, government, and industry. Among the more prominent was the Landgrave Robert Daniell, of a Norman family of Latin heritage and royal descent. He served as Governor of North and South Carolina and provided counsel on the final revision of the Fundamental Constitutions of Carolina that became the law of that colony. Formerly a sea captain, he was both a Lieutenant General and Vice Admiral and led the British forces during the Siege of Saint Augustine, among other military actions of historical significance. Another particularly distinguished colonial ancestor of the family was Michiel Jansen van Vreeland. He served as a magistrate and was also a member of the Assembly of Nine Men, the governing body of the New Netherlands in present-day New York. Today the head of the household is His Holiness and Eminence Papa Rutherford I, Prince of the Romans and Grand Duke of Ruthenia. His Holiness is the Florentine-Roman Supreme Pontiff, as pastoral leader of both the Anglican Rite and the Gallican Rite of the Catholic Church. He is married to Her Imperial and Royal Majesty the Grand Duchess Hanna Alexandrovna, Princess of the Romans and Grand Duchess of Ruthenia. The parents of the Florentine-Roman Papa are Their Imperial & Royal Highnesses the Grand Duke Ralph and the Grand Duchess Marianne, Grand Prince and Grand Princess of Etruria.

Coat of Arms

The principal coat of arms of the household is described as follows: Quarterly of six: 1) The Coadjutorship of Rome; 2) Of Etruria, being of Parma and the Roman Duchy of Santa Croce; 3) Spanish Ivrea, being of Barcelona quartered with Castile y León, with France in pretense; 4) Würzburg, with the ecclesiastical electorate of Würzburg in pretense with an electoral bonnet of the Holy Roman Empire;

5) Of ancient Etruria, being Lorraine quartered with Bar; and 6) Quarterly, of Florence, Sainte Animie, Valais, and Daniell; in pretense, of the Principality of Santa Croce (the Crusader States, Normandy and Flanders, Spain and Ruthenia, and David), with Johnson-Ivrea in pretense thereupon.

The shield is displayed upon a black imperial double-headed eagle, with gold arms and beaks and red tongues. Each head is crowned with a Roman imperial crown. The motto is "Honos Ministerium Fides," being translated as "Honor, Service, and Loyalty." The arms may also be displayed upon a gold imperial mantle with gold eagles thereupon, with red panels, and with red crosses of Saint Stephen on the pavilion.

As used by the Florentine-Roman Papa, the arms are surmounted by the pontifical insignia, with the shield encircled by the collars of the Supreme Florentine-Roman Order of Christ and the Pontifical Order of the Eagle. This also represents the entire household. As used by the Princess of Rome, the arms are surmounted by the gold Roman imperial crown. By the Grand Dukes and Grand Duchesses of the line, the arms may be surmounted by a silver Roman imperial crown.

Titles of the Flor.-Rom. Papa
(Source: Almanac of Würzburg)

Florentine Archfather
Grand Pontiff of the Anglican Rite of the Universal Church
Supreme Pastor of the Anglican Rite of the Universal Church
Legate of Jesus Christ
Prince of the Romans
Coadjutor of Rome
Anglican Patriarch of Rome
Anglo-Roman Archbishop & Metropolitan of the Province of Aquileia
Anglo-Roman Primate of Italy
Custodian of the Apostolic See of St. Mark at Aquileia
Roman Caesar, Archprince, and Bishop of St. Stephen
Titular Archbishop and Metropolitan of Leontopoli
Cardinal Deacon i.p.c. of Santa Maria Antiqua
Cardinal Prince of Florence
Prince Archbishop and Elector of Würzburg
Duke of Franconia
Grand Duke and titular King of Ruthenia
Archregent of Etruria in the Holy Roman Empire
Prince of Galicia-Volhynia, Vladimir, Novgorod, Peremyshl, and Belz
Imperial Lord of Italy, Naples, Walsingham, and the Floridas
Titular Bishop of Iconium
Assistant at the Pontifical Throne of the Bishop of Rome
Prince of Etruria and Santa Croce
Prince Elector of the Holy Roman Empire

Select Honours of the Flor.-Rom. Papa

Florentine-Roman Knight of Christ

Knight Grand Cross of the Religious and Military Order of Anna Alexandrovna

Bailiff Grand Cross of the Pontifical Order of the Eagle

Knight of the Order of Saints George and Olga

Knight of the Florentine-Roman Order of the Golden Spur

Knight Grand Collar of the Florentine-Roman Order of Saint Pius IX

Knight Grand Cross of the Florentine-Roman Order of Saint Gregory the Great

Knight Grand Cross of the Florentine-Roman Order of Saint Sylvester

Knight Grand Cross of the Order of the Pontifical States

Member of the Pontifical Order of Merit

Knight Grand Cross of the Imperial Teutonic Order

Knight Grand Collar of Justice of the Crown Order of Westphalia

Knight of the Order of Concordia

Noble Companion of the Noble Company of the Court of Saint Mary of Walsingham

Companion with Amethysts of the Order of the Star of Coberly v. Reichenberg

Knight Grand Cross of Justice of the Ruthenian Order of St. Lazarus of Jerusalem

Knight Companion of the Imperial Order of St. Constantine

Knight Commander with Star of the Order of St. Stanislas

Knight with Chain of Honour of the Order of the Iron Crown, Napoleonic Honour Guard

Select Ancestors

Byzantine Roman Emperors

Isaac II Angelos

Alexios I Komnenos

Michael II

Theophilus

Michael III

Leo VI

Constantine VII

Romanos II

Romanos IV Diogenes

Imperial Kingdom of Italy

Hugh d'Arles, King of Italy

Berengar I, King of Italy

Berengar II, King of Italy

Adalbert, King of Italy

Spain & Sicily

Ramón Berenguer III, Count of Barcelona and Gévaudan

Ramón Berenguer IV, Count of Barcelona

Alfonso II, King of Aragón

Urraca, Queen of Castile y León, Empress of All Spain

Alfonso VII, King of Castile y León, Emperor of All Spain

Sancho III, King of Castile

Alfonso VIII, King of Castile

James I, King of Aragón

Roger II, King of Sicily

Peter II, King of Aragón

Peter III, King of Aragón, King of Sicily

Federico III, King of Sicily

Manfred II, King of Sicily

Kievan Rus (Rurikid Dynasty, Grand Princes of Kiev)

Vladimir the Great	Sviatopolk II
Yaroslav the Wise	Sviatoslav II
Mstislav I	Oleg I, Prince of Chernigov
Mstislav II	Sviatoslav III
Iziaslav II	Vsevolod IV
Vladimir II	Rostislav I
Vsevolod I	Roman I
Vsevolod II	Mstislav III

Kings of Russia (Romanovich Dynasty (Rurikid))

Roman the Great, Tsar and Autocrat of all Rus', Grand Prince of Kiev, Prince of Novgorod and Halych

Danylo Romanovich, King of Russia (Ruthenia), Grand Prince of Kiev

Lev I, King of Russia (Ruthenia), Grand Prince of Kiev

Yuri I, King of Russia (Ruthenia), Grand Prince of Kiev

Grand Dukes of Lithuania

Butvydas	Gediminas
Dangerutis	

Dukes of Burgundy

Robert I	Odo II
Odo I	Hugh III
Hugh II	Odo III

Hugh IV

Robert II

John I

Philip II

Kings of Hungary

Béla I

Géza I

Béla II

Géza II

Béla III

Andrew II

Béla IV

Stephen V

Kings of France

Robert II

Henri I

Philip I

Louis VI

Louis VII

Louis VII

Louis IX

Philip III

Philip IV

Philip V

Philip VI

Jean II

Charles V

Charles VI

Holy Roman Emperors

Charlemagne

Conrad II

Henry III

Henry IV

Henry VI

Henry VII

Friedrich I

Friedrich II

Otto II

Louis IV

Arles and Ivrea

Bosone, King of Lower Provence and Vice-King of Italy in the Holy
Roman Empire

Bosone d'Arles, Margrave of Tuscany

Otto-William (Ivrea), Count of Burgundy

Reginald I (Ivrea), Count of Burgundy

Renaud I (Ivrea), Count of Burgundy

William I (Ivrea), Count of Burgundy

Stephen I (Ivrea), Count of Burgundy

William III (Ivrea), Count of Mâcon

Stephen II (Ivrea), Count of Auxonne

Stephen III (Ivrea), Count of Auxonne

England and Scotland

William the Conqueror, Duke of Normandy, King of England

Henry I, King of England

Henry II, King of England

Henry III, King of England

John, King of England

Richard "Strongbow" de Clare, 1st Earl of Pembroke

James I, King of Scotland

James II, King of Scotland

James III, King of Scotland

James IV, King of Scotland

Edward III (Plantagenet), King of England

John of Gaunt (Plantagenet), Duke of Lancaster

Edward I "Longshanks," King of England

Edward II, King of England

Edward III, King of England

Edward IV, King of England

Alfred the Great, King of Wessex

Matilda, Holy Roman Empress, Queen of England

Warin de Lisle, Baron Lisle

Robert, Landgrave Daniell

Ireland

Brian Boru, High King of Ireland

Donnchad, King of Munster

Dermot II McMurrough, King of Leinster

Gévaudan/Sainte Animie

Richard I de Milau, Viscount of Gévaudan

Richard II de Milau, Viscount of Gévaudan

Berenger de Milau, Viscount of Gévaudan

Gilbert, Count of Gévaudan

Flanders, Hainaut, and Brabant

Robert I, Count of Namur

Albert I, Count of Namur

Robert I, Lord of Béthune

Albert II, Count of Namur

Robert II, Lord of Béthune

Conrad I, Count of Luxembourg

Albert III, Count of Namur

Robert III, Lord of Béthune

Arnulf II, Count of Flanders

Godfrey I, Count of Namur

Robert IV, Lord of Béthune

Arnulf I, Count of Flanders

Baldwin III, Count of Flanders

Baldwin IV, Count of Flanders

William I, Lord of Béthune

Baldwin V, Count of Flanders

Robert V, Lord of Béthune

Baldwin VI, Count of Flanders

Margaret I, Countess of Flanders (House of Metz)

Baldwin II, Count of Hainaut, called of Jerusalem

Henry I, Duke of Brabant

Henry II, Duke of Brabant

Margaret II, Countess of Flanders

Bohemia *(Premyslid Dynasty)*

Borivoj I, Duke of Bohemia

Wratislaus I, Duke of Bohemia

Boleslaus I, Duke of Bohemia

Boleslaus II, Duke of Bohemia

Oldrich, Duke of Bohemia

Bretislaus I, Duke of Bohemia

Wratislaus II, King of Bohemia

Constantinople

Peter II de Courtenay, Latin Emperor of Constantinople

Baldwin I, Latin Emperor of Constantinople

Jean de Brienne, King of Jerusalem, Latin Emperor of Constantinople

Jerusalem

Baldwin II, King of Jerusalem (House of Rethel)

Fulk, King of Jerusalem (House of Anjou)

Jean de Brienne, King of Jerusalem, Latin Emperor of Constantinople (House of Brienne)

Amalric I, King of Jerusalem (House of Anjou)

Isabella I, Queen of Jerusalem (House of Anjou)

Aimery de Lusignan, King of Cyprus (House of Lusignan)

Hugh I de Lusignan, King of Cyprus (House of Lusignan)

HERALDRY & FLAGS

**Greater Coat of Arms of
the Pontifical Florentine-Roman House
of Johnson-Ivrea-Italia-Barcelona**

Quarter 1: Coadjutorship of Rome, being also the arms of the Most
Holy Patriarchal Basilica of Santa Maria Antiqua in Rome.

Quarter 2: Arms of Etruria (modern), being the arms of Parma
mar-shaled with the Roman ducal arms of Santa Croce.

Quarter 3: Spanish Ivrea, being Barcelona quartered with Castile y León, with France in pretense.

Quarter 4: The arms of Würzburg, with ecclesiastical Würzburg in pretense.

Quarter 5: The ancient arms of Etruria, being the quartered arms of Lorraine and Bar.

Quarter 6: Quarterly, 1) Florence, 2) Sainte Animie, 3) Valais, and 4) Daniell.

In pretense overall, the arms of the Principality of Santa Croce. In that shield, the cross flory of the first quarter is of the Crusader States; the second quarter is of Normandy and Flanders; the third quarter is of Spain and Ruthenia (and further is a variation on the lion of Judah, representing that ancient tribe); and the fourth quarter represents King David.

The shield is placed upon the dual cross of the Pontifical Order of the Eagle and further augmented with the collar of the Order of the Eagle, and the collars of the Noble Company of St. Mary of Walsingham and the Crown Order of Westphalia. Behind the shield are also crossed two batons of the Sovereign and Grand Master of the Order of the Eagle and the flag of the Imperial Kingdom of Italy and the flag of the Kingdom of Etruria. Upon the two golden helms are placed the Patriarchal Crowned Mitre and the family crest, being a red fleur-de-lis charged with a sword, issuant from a chapeau. From the helms issue mantling in gold and ermine. A gold Roman imperial crown is placed above. The shield is placed upon a black imperial eagle with gold beaks and arms and red tounges. Below the shield are four small shields, being of Rome, Trier, Mainz, and Köln. For supporters are two white rampant horses representing Saxony, i.e., the Saxon steed, holding in their mouths a green slip of oak.

The achievement is placed upon a mantle with pavilion. The mantle is gold and decorated with golden eagles. The pavilion is gold and decorated with red crosses of St. Stephen, and with panels in red. Behind the pavilion is an armourial array, as well as the full Pontifical Insignia, being the key of St. Peter and the sword of Sts. Mark and Paul, with the Papal Tiara, which surmounts the pavilion.

For outer supporters are two ombrellini supported by two angels in white robes with a red sash and gold fringe. The dexter ombrellino is decorated with a red crosses of St. Stephen and is atop three stones representing the martyrdom of St. Stephen. The other is decorated with blue crosses of Mary Immaculate and is a top three lilies, representing Our Lady of Walsingham. Behind the entire achievement on the sides are, two on each side, the civil flag of the Stato Pontificio. On vertical poles topped with the Teutonic cross, one flag on each side, is the military flag of the Anglican Patriarchate, viz., the Florentine Triple Cross.

**Middle Coat of Arms of
the Pontifical Florentine-Roman House
of Johnson-Ivrea-Italia-Barcelona**

The shield upon the imperial eagle, with each head crowned
with a gold Roman imperial crown,
upon the same mantle as in the greater arms.

Imperial Eagle of the Florentine-Roman Papa

Imperial Eagle of the Princess of the Romans

Arms of the Anglican Patriarchate of Rome
and Imperial Kingdom of Italy

The coat of arms of the Patriarchate consists of the Johnson-Ivrea shield upon a black doppeladler, surmounted by the papal tiara and crossed key and sword.

Small Imperial Eagle

The small imperial eagle, which represents the Pontifical Household and may additionally be used by all Grand Dukes thereof, is a black doppeladler without coat of arms, with a gold Roman imperial crown on each head, and surmounted by the pontifical insignia.

Pontifical Grand Ducal Crown

This crown, as well as a black doppeladler, may be used by the Grand Dukes of Rome. It is identical to the gold variant, with the mitres instead in silver.

Civil Flag of the Stato Pontificio

Military Flag of the Stato Pontificio

Banner of Christus Omnipotens
*The banner of the Church. When flown or carried, it
precedes all other flags, banners, and standards.*

Military Flag of the Anglican Patriarchate
(Florentine Triple Cross)

Maritime Ensign of the Archfather

Boat and Car Pennant of the Archfather

Civil (State) Flag of the Imperial Kingdom of Italy

Standard of His Holiness and Eminence the Holy Father

The flag is used to represent the Florentine-Roman Papa and indicates his presence.

Banner of the Pontifical Household

The banner of the Pontifical Household is a rectangular yellow flag with a border of alternating triangles in red, yellow, blue, and white. At the corners are four red St. Stephen crosses. In the centre is the imperial eagle (version with shield). It may be flown after the personal standard by the Papa, Princess of the Romans, and the Grand Dukes/Duchesses.

Standard of the Princess of the Romans

Standard of the Grand Dukes and Grand Duchess of Rome

This standard represents all the Grand Dukes and Grand Duchesses. If they are entitled to another standard according to title, then this standard flies above it.

APOSTOLIC & TEMPORAL SUCCESSION

The following summarizes the main lines of Apostolic and Temporal Succession of the Florentine-Roman household.

LEONINE AND IMPERIAL APOSTOLIC SUCCESSION

Roman Catholic
(Pope Leo X, Prince of Florence - I)
Genealogical Addendum

Saint Louis IX, King of France
|
Robert, Count of Clermont
|
Peter I, Duke of Bourbon
|
Jean VI, Count d'Haricourt = Catherine de Bourbon
|
Marguerite d'Haricourt = Jean d'Estouteville, Lord of
Vallemont, Grand Chamberlain
of France
|
Guillaume Cardinal d'Estouteville, O.S.B.,
Archbishop of Rouen, Cardinal Bishop of Ostia

Episcopal Succession

Pope Sixtus IV
Pope St. Julius II
Raffaele Cardinal Sansone Riario, Cardinal Bishop of Ostia
Pope St. Leo X
Pope Paul III

Francesco Cardinal Pisani, Cardinal Bishop of Ostia
Alfonso Cardinal Gesualdo di Conza,
Archbishop of Naples, Cardinal Bishop of Ostia
Pope Clement VIII
Pietro Cardinal Aldobrandini,
Archbishop of Ravenna
Laudivio Cardinal Zacchia,
Bishop of Corneto e Montefiascone
Antonio Marcello Cardinal Barberini,
Bishop of Senigallia
Marcantonio Cardinal Franciotti, Bishop of Lucca
Giambattista Cardinal Spada,
Patriarch of Constanstinople
Carlo Cardinal Pio di Savoia, Bishop of Ferrara
Ercole Visconti, Titular Archbishop of Tamiathis
Wilhelm Egon Cardinal von Fürstenberg, Bishop of Strasbourg,
Prince of Fürstenberg-Heiligenberg
Armand-Gaston-Maximilien Cardinal de Rohan de Soubise,
Bishop of Strasbourg
Louis-François du Plessis de Mornay, O.F.M. Cap.,
Bishop of Quebec
Dominique-Marie Varlet, Bishop of Baghdad

Roman Catholic
(Pope St. Leo X, Prince of Florence - II)

Juan Cardinal Pardo de Tavera, Archbishop of Toledo
Antoine Cardinal Perrenot de Granvella,
Archbishop of Besançon
Francisco Cardinal Pacheco de Toledo,
Archbishop of Burgos
Pope Leo XI (Archbishop of Florence)
Pietro Cardinal Aldobrandini,
Archbishop of Ravenna
Laudivio Cardinal Zacchia,
Bishop of Corneto e Montefiascone
Antonio Marcello Cardinal Barberini,
Bishop of Senigallia
Marcantonio Cardinal Franciotti, Bishop of Lucca
Giambattista Cardinal Spada,
Patriarch of Constanstinople

Carlo Cardinal Pio di Savoia, Bishop of Ferrara
Ercole Visconti, Titular Archbishop of Tamiathis
Wilhelm Egon Cardinal von Fürstenberg, Bishop of Strasbourg,
Prince of Fürstenberg-Heiligenberg
Armand-Gaston-Maximilien Cardinal de Rohan de Soubise,
Bishop of Strasbourg
Louis-François du Plessis de Mornay, O.F.M. Cap.,
Bishop of Quebec
Dominique-Marie Varlet, Bishop of Baghdad

Roman Catholic (Pope St. Leo X - Holy Roman Empire Line - I)
Pope St. Leo X
Pope Clement VII (Archbishop of Florence)
Antonio Cardinal Sanseverino, O.S.Io.Hieros., Archbishop of Taranto
Giovanni Michele Cardinal Saraceni
Pope Pius V
Iñigo Cardinal Avalos de Aragón, O.S.
Scipione Cardinal Gonzaga, Patriarch of Jerusalem
Blondus de Montealto, Patriarch of Jerusalem
Pope Urban VIII
Cosimo Cardinal de Torres, Archbishop of Monreale
Francesco Maria Cardinal Brancaccio
Miguel Juan Balaguer Camarasa, O.S.Io.Hieros., Bishop of Malta
Pope Alexander VII
Max Heinrich von Bayern,
Prince Archbishop and Elector of Köln in the Holy Roman Empire
Johann Heinrich von Anethan,
Auxiliary Bishop of the Electorate of Köln
in the Holy Roman Empire
Wilhelm Egon Cardinal von Fürstenberg, Bishop of Strasbourg,
Prince of Fürstenberg-Heiligenberg
Armand-Gaston-Maximilien Cardinal de Rohan de Soubise,
Bishop of Strasbourg
Louis-François du Plessis de Mornay, O.F.M. Cap.,
Bishop of Quebec
Dominique-Marie Varlet, Bishop of Baghdad

Roman Catholic (Pope St. Leo X - Holy Roman Empire Line - II)

Max Heinrich von Bayern, Prince Archbishop and Elector of Köln
    in the Holy Roman Empire (*See section above, HRE-I*)

Johann Heinrich von Anethan,
    Auxiliary Bishop of the Electorate of Köln in the Holy Roman
    Empire

Johann Hugo von Orsbeck, Prince Archbishop and Elector of Trier
    in the Holy Roman Empire

Maximilian Burmann, Auxiliary Bishop of the Electorate of Trier in
    the Holy Roman Empire

Wilhelm Egon Cardinal von Fürstenberg, Bishop of Strasbourg,
Prince of Fürstenberg-Heiligenberg

Armand-Gaston-Maximilien Cardinal de Rohan de Soubise, Bishop
    of Strasbourg

Louis-François du Plessis de Mornay, O.F.M. Cap., Bishop of
    Quebec

Dominique-Marie Varlet, Bishop of Baghdad

Roman Catholic (Pope St. Leo X - Holy Roman Empire Line - III)

Giovanni Antonio Cardinal Serbelloni, Cardinal Bishop of Ostia

Saint Charles (Cardinal) Borromeo, Archbishop of Milan

Gabriele Cardinal Paleotti, Archbishop of Bologna

Ludovico Cardinal de Torres, Archbishop of Monreale

Giovanni Garzia Cardinal Mellini, Archbishop of Imola

Antonio Albergati, Bishop of Bisceglie

Gereon Otto von Gutmann zu Sobernheim, Auxiliary Bishop of the
    Electorate of Köln in the Holy Roman Empire

Johannes Pelking, O.F.M. Conv., Auxiliary Bishop of Paderborn

Wolther Heinrich von Strevesdorff, O.E.S.A., Auxiliary Bishop of
    the Electorate of Mainz in the Holy Roman Empire

Johann Philipp von Schönborn, Prince Archbishop and Elector of
    Mainz in the Holy Roman Empire, Prince Bishop of Würzburg

Stephan Weinberger, Auxiliary Bishop of Würzburg in the Holy
    Roman Empire

Peter Philipp von Dernbach, Prince Bishop of Würzburg in the
    Holy Roman Empire

Damian Hartard von Leyen-Hohengeroldseck, Prince Archbishop
    and Elector of Mainz in the Holy Roman Empire

Adolph Gottfried Volusius, Auxiliary Bishop of the Electorate of
    Mainz in the Holy Roman Empire

Johann Heinrich von Anethan, Auxiliary Bishop of the Electorate of
  Köln in the Holy Roman Empire
Johann Hugo von Orsbeck, Prince Archbishop and Elector of Trier
  in the Holy Roman Empire
Maximilian Burmann, Auxiliary Bishop of the Electorate of Trier in
  the Holy Roman Empire
Wilhelm Egon Cardinal von Fürstenberg, Bishop of Strasbourg,
  Prince of Fürstenberg-Heiligenberg
Armand-Gaston-Maximilien Cardinal de Rohan de Soubise, Bishop
  of Strasbourg
Louis-François du Plessis de Mornay, O.F.M. Cap., Bishop of
  Quebec
Dominique-Marie Varlet, Bishop of Baghdad

Principal Sources:
Les Ordinations Épiscopales, Year 1719, Number 3
Les Ordinations Épiscopales, Year 1714, Number 8
Hierarchia Catholica, Volume 5
The Cardinals of the Holy Roman Church, 1686
Die Bischöfe des Heiligen Römischen Reiches
Les Ordinations Épiscopales, Year 1678, Number 23
Les Nonciatures Apostoliques Permanentes
Les Ordinations Épiscopales, Year 1625, Number 2
Les Ordinations Épiscopales, Year 1604, Number 27
Le Petit Episcopologe, Issue 176, Number 14
The Cardinals of the Holy Roman Church, 20 Sep 1493
Hierarchia Catholica, Volume 3
Les Ordinations Épiscopales, Year 1519, Number 10
Le Petit Épiscopologe, Issue 176, Number 14
The Cardinals of the Holy Roman Church, 10 Dec 1477
Episcopologio Español, Volume 1500
Les Ordinations Épiscopales, Year 1504, Number 4
The Cardinals of the Holy Roman Church, 18 Sep 1467
Le Petit Épiscopologe, Issue 205, Number 16
The Cardinals of the Holy Roman Church, 18 Dec 1439
Le Petit Épiscopologe, Issue 205, Number 16
Hierarchia Catholica, Volume 2

EASTERN RITE LINES OF SUCCESSION

Russian Orthodox (from Nikon, Patriarch of Moscow and All Rus';
  and Sergius Starogrodsky, Metropolitan of Nizhni-Novgorod,
  Patriarch of Moscow and All Rus')

Syrian Antiochene (from Mar Ignatius III, Syrian Orthodox Patriarch of Antioch)

Syrian Malabarese (from Mar Ignatius Peter III, Patriarch of Antioch)

Syrian Gallican (from Mar Julius, Metropolitan of Goa; Mar Athanasius, Metropolitan of Angamaly; and Mar Gregorios, Metropolitan of Niranam)

Syro Chaldean (from Mar Shimum XVIII, Patriarch of Seleucia-Ctesiphon and Catholicos of the East; Mar Abdese-Antonios, Metropolitan of Malabar; and Mar Basileus, Metropolitan of India, Ceylon, Mylapore, Socotra, and Messina)

Chaldean Uniate (from Mar Emmanuel Thomas II, Patriarch of Babylon)

Armenian Uniate (from Archbishop Charchorunian, consecreated under the reign of Patriarch Antonios Peter IX)

Greek Melkite Uniate (from Athanasius Sawoya, Greek Melkite Archbishop of Beyrouth and Gebeil in Syria)

Russo-Syriac (from Archbishop Evdokim, Archbishop of Nizhny-Novgorod and Archbishop of the Aleutians)

ROMAN CATHOLIC

+ Jesus Christ
1. St. Peter the Apostle
2. St. Linus
3. St. Anacletus
4. St. Clement I
5. St. Evaristus
6. St. Alexander I
7. St. Sixtus I
8. St. Telephorus
9. St. Hyginus
10. St. Pius I
11. St. Anicetus
12. St. Soter
13. St. Eleutherius
14. St. Victor I
15. St. Zephyrinus
16. St. Callistus I
17. St. Urban I
18. St. Pontian
19. St. Anterus

20. St. Fabian
21. St. Cornelius
22. St. Lucius I
23. St. Stephen I
24. St. Sixtus II
25. St. Dionysius
26. St. Felix I
27. St. Eutychian
28. St. Caius
29. St. Mercellinus
30. St. Marcellus I
31. St. Eusebius
32. St. Miltiades
33. St. Sylvester
34. St. Mark
35. St. Julius I
36. St. Liberius
37. St. Damascus
38. St. Siricius
39. St. Anastasius I
40. St. Innocent I
41. St. Zosimus
42. St. Boniface I
43. St. Celestine I
44. St. Sixtus III
45. St. Leo I "The Great"
46. St. Hilarus
47. St. Simplicius
48. St. Felix III
49. St. Gelasius I
50. Anastasius II
51. St. Symmachus
52. St. Hormisdas
53. St. John I
54. St. Felix IV
55. Boniface II
56. St. John II
57. St. Agapitus I
58. St. Silverius
59. Vigilius

60. Palagius I
61. John III
62. Benedict I
63. Pelagius II
64. St. Gregory I "The Great"
65. Sabinianus
66. Boniface III
67. St. Boniface IV
68. St. Adeodatus I
69. Boniface V
70. Honorius I
71. Severinus
72. John IV
73. Theodore I
74. St. Martin I
75. St. Eugenius I
76. St. Vitalian
77. Adeodatus II
78. Donus
79. St. Agatho
80. St. Leo II
81. St. Benedict II
82. John V
83. Conon
84. St. Sergius I
85. John VI
86. John VII
87. Sissinius
88. Constantine
89. St. Gregory II
90. St. Gregory III
91. St. Zacharias
92. Stephen II
93. St. Paul I
94. Stephen III
95. Adrian I
96. St. Leo III
97. Stephen IV
98. St. Paschal I
99. Eugenius II

100. Valentine
101. Gregory IV
102. Sergius II
103. St. Leo IV
104. Benedict III
105. St. Nicholas I
106. Adrian II
107. John VIII
108. Marinus I
109. St. Adrian III
110. Stephen V
111. Formosus
112. Boniface VI
113. Stephen VI
114. Romanus
115. Theodore II
116. John IX
117. Benedict IV
118. Leo V
119. Sergius III
120. Anastasius III
121. Lando
122. John X
123. Leo VI
124. John XI
125. Leo VII
126. Stephen VII
127. Stephen VIII
128. Marinus II
129. Agapetus II
130. John XII
131. Leo VIII
132. Benedict V
133. John XIII
134. Benedict VI
135. Benedict VII
136. John XIV
137. John XV
138. Gregory V
139. Sylvester II

140. John XVII
141. John XVIII
142. Sergius IV
143. Benedict VIII
144. John XIX
145. Benedict IX
146. Sylvester III
147. Gregory VI
148. Clement II
149. Damasus II
150. St. Leo IX
151. Victor II
152. Stephen IX
153. Nicholas II
154. Alexander II
155. St. Gregory VII
156. Blessed Victor III
157. Blessed Urban II
158. Paschal II
159. Gelasiur II
160. Callistus II
161. Honorius II
162. Innocent II
163. Celestine II
164. Lucius II
165. Blessed Eugenius III
166. Anastasius IV
167. Adrian IV
168. Alexander III
169. Lucius III
170. Urban III
171. Gregory VIII
172. Clement III
173. Celestine III
174. Innocent III
175. Honorius III
176. Gregory IX
177. Celestine IV
178. Innocent IV
179. Alexander IV

180. Urban IV
181. Clement IV
182. Blessed Gregory X
183. Blessed Innocent V
184. Adrian V
185. John XXI
186. Nicholas III
187. Martin IV
188. Honorius IV
189. Nicholas IV
190. St. Celestine V
191. Boniface VIII
192. Blessed Benedict XI
193. Clement V
194. John XXII & Nicholas V
195. Benedict XII
196. Clement VI
197. Innocent VI
198. Blessed Urban V
199. Gregory XI
200. Urban VI
201. Boniface IX
202. Innocent VII
203. Gregory XII
204. Martin V
205. Eugenius IV

206. Nicholas V
207. Callistus III
208. Pius II
209. Paul II
210. Sixtus IV
211. Innocent VIII
212. Alexander VI
213. Pius III
214. St. Julius II
215. St. Leo X
216. Adrian VI
217. Clement VII
218. Paul III
219. Julius III
220. Marcellus II
221. Paul IV
222. St. Pius IV
223. St. Pius V
224. Gregory XIII
225. Sixtus V
226. Urban VII
227. Gregory XIV
228. Innocent IX
229. Clement VIII
230. Leo XI
231. Paul V

232. Gregory XV   St. Pius V (see above)
233. Urban VIII   ↓
234. Innocent X   234a. Cosimo Cardinal de Torres
235. Alexander VII   235a. Ludovico Cardinal Ludovisi
    (see also HRE-I above)   235b. Luigi Cardinal Caetani
235c. Giovanni Battista Scanaroli
236. Antonio Cardinal Barberini (nephew of Urban VIII)

ANTIOCH

+	Jesus Christ	37.	Severius the Great
1.	St. Peter the Apostle	38.	Sergius
↓		39.	Domnus III
2.	Evodius	40.	Anastasius
3.	Ignatius I, Martyr	41.	Gregory I
4.	Earon	42.	Paul II
5.	Cornelius	43.	Patra
6.	Eados	44.	Domnus IV
7.	Theophilus	45.	Julianus
8.	Maximinus	46.	Athanasius I
9.	Seraphim	47.	Julianus II
10.	Asclepiades, Martyr	48.	Theodorus I
11.	Philip	49.	Severus
12.	Zebinus	50.	Athanasius II
13.	Babylos, Martyr	51.	Julianus II
14.	Fabius	52.	Elias I
15.	Demetrius	53.	Athanasius III
16.	Paul I	54.	Evanius I
17.	Domnus I	55.	Gervasius I
18.	Tomotheus	56.	Joseph
19.	Cyrilus	57.	Cyriacus
20.	Tyrantus	58.	Dionysius I
21.	Vitalius	59.	John III
22.	Philogonius	60.	Ignatius II
23.	Eustachius	61.	Theodisius
24.	Paulinus	62.	Dionysius II
25.	Philabinus	63.	John IV
26.	Evagrinus	64.	Basilius I
27.	Phosphorius	65.	John V
28.	Alexander	66.	Evanius II
29.	John I	67.	Dionysius III
30.	Theodotus	68.	Abraham I
31.	Domnus II	69.	John VI
32.	Maximus	70.	Athanasius IV
33.	Accacius	71.	John VII
34.	Martyrius	72.	Dionysius IV
35.	Peter II	73.	Theodorus II
36.	Philadius	74.	Athanasius V

75.	John VIII		101.	Ignatius Noah
76.	Basilius II		102.	Ignatius Jesus I
77.	Abdoone		103.	Ignatius Jacob I
78.	Dionysius V		104.	Ignatius David I
79.	Evanius III		105.	Ignatius Abdullah
80.	Dionysius VI		106.	Ignatius Neamathalak
81.	Athanasius VI		107.	Ignatius David II
82.	John IX		108.	Ignatius Philathus
83.	Athanasius VII		109.	Ignatius Abdullah II
84.	Michael I "The Great"		110.	Ignatius Cadhai
			111.	Ignatius Simeon
85.	Athanasius VIII		112.	Ignatius Jesus II
86.	Michael II		113.	Ignatius Amessiah
87.	John X		114.	Ignatius Cabeed
88.	Ignatius III		115.	Ignatius Gervasius II
89.	Dionysius VII		116.	Ignatius Isaac
90.	John XI		117.	Ignatius Siccarablak
91.	Ignatius IV		118.	Ignatius Gervasius III
92.	Philamus		119.	Ignatius Gervasius IV
93.	Ignatius Beruhid		120.	Ignatius Mathias
94.	Ignatius Ismael		121.	Ignatius Behanan II
95.	Ignatius Basilius III		122.	Ignatius Jonas
96.	Ignatius Abraham II		123.	Ignatius Gervasius V
97.	Ignatius Basilius IV		124.	Ignatius Elias II
98.	Ignatius Behanan I		125.	Ignatius Jacob II
99.	Ignatius Kalojih		126.	Ignatius Peter III
100.	Ignatius John XII			

ROMAN CATHOLIC
(additional lines)

Via...
Scipione Cardinal Rebiba, Cardinal Bishop of Sabina
Benedict XIII
Benedict XIV
Clement XIII
Leo XIII

MELKITE CATHOLIC

Athanasius Sawoya, Greek Melkite Archbishop of Beyrouth and
Gebeil in Syria

Antoine Joseph Aneed, Exarch of the Greek Melkite Rite in the
United States of America

ANGLICAN

+Jesus Christ+ to:

1. Marco Antonio de Dominis, Archbishop of Spalato
2. George Monteigne, Bishop of Lincoln, later Bishop of London
3. William Laud, Bishop of St. David, later Archbishop of
   Canterbury
4. Brian Duppa, Bishop of Chichester
5. Gilbert Sheldon, Bishop of London, later Archbishop of
   Canterbury
6. Henry Compton, Bishop of Oxford, later Bishop of London
7. William Sancroft, Archbishop of Canterbury
8. Thomas White, Bishop of Peterborough
9. George Hickes, Suffragan Bishop of Thetford
10. James Gadderer, Bishop of Aberdeen
11. Thomas Rattray, Bishop of Dunkeld
12. William Falconer, Bishop of Caithness
13. Robert Kilgour, Bishop of Aberdeen
14. Samuel Seabury, Bishop of Connecticut
15. Thomas J. Claggett, Bishop of Maryland
16. Edward Bass, Bishop of Massachusetts
17. Abraham Jarvis, Bishop of Connecticut
18. Alexander Viets Griswold, Bishop of the Eastern Diocese
19. Henry U. Onderdonk, Bishop of Pennsylvania
20. Samuel A. McCoskry, Bishop of Michigan
21. William E. McLaren, Bishop of Chicago
22. William Montgomery Brown, Bishop of Arkansas

TEMPORAL SUCCESSION

1. St. Peter (32-67)
2. St. Linus (67-76)
3. St. Anacletus (Cletus) (76-88)
4. St. Clement I (88-97)

5. St. Evaristus (97-105)
6. St. Alexander I (105-115)
7. St. Sixtus I (115-125) *Also called Xystus I*
8. St. Telesphorus (125-136)
9. St. Hyginus (136-140)
10. St. Pius I (140-155)
11. St. Anicetus (155-166)
12. St. Soter (166-175)
13. St. Eleutherius (175-189)
14. St. Victor I (189-199)
15. St. Zephyrinus (199-217)
16. St. Callistus I (217-22)
17. St. Urban I (222-30)
18. St. Pontian (230-35)
19. St. Anterus (235-36)
20. St. Fabian (236-50)
21. St. Cornelius (251-53)
22. St. Lucius I (253-54)
23. St. Stephen I (254-257)
24. St. Sixtus II (257-258)
25. St. Dionysius (260-268)
26. St. Felix I (269-274)
27. St. Eutychian (275-283)
28. St. Caius (283-296)
29. St. Marcellinus (296-304)
30. St. Marcellus I (308-309)
31. St. Eusebius (309 or 310)
32. St. Miltiades (311-14)
33. St. Sylvester I (314-35)
34. St. Marcus (336)
35. St. Julius I (337-52)
36. Liberius (352-66)
37. St. Damasus I (366-84)
38. St. Siricius (384-99)
39. St. Anastasius I (399-401)
40. St. Innocent I (401-17)
41. St. Zosimus (417-18)
42. St. Boniface I (418-22)
43. St. Celestine I (422-32)
44. St. Sixtus III (432-40)

45. St. Leo I (the Great) (440-61)
46. St. Hilarius (461-68)
47. St. Simplicius (468-83)
48. St. Felix III (II) (483-92)
49. St. Gelasius I (492-96)
50. Anastasius II (496-98)
51. St. Symmachus (498-514)
52. St. Hormisdas (514-23)
53. St. John I (523-26)
54. St. Felix IV (III) (526-30)
55. Boniface II (530-32)
56. John II (533-35)
57. St. Agapetus I (535-36)
58. St. Silverius (536-37)
59. Vigilius (537-55)
60. Pelagius I (556-61)
61. John III (561-74)
62. Benedict I (575-79)
63. Pelagius II (579-90)
64. St. Gregory I (the Great) (590-604)
65. Sabinian (604-606)
66. Boniface III (607)
67. St. Boniface IV (608-15)
68. St. Deusdedit (Adeodatus I) (615-18)
69. Boniface V (619-25)
70. Honorius I (625-38)
71. Severinus (640)
72. John IV (640-42)
73. Theodore I (642-49)
74. St. Martin I (649-55)
75. St. Eugene I (655-57)
76. St. Vitalian (657-72)
77. Adeodatus (II) (672-76)
78. Donus (676-78)
79. St. Agatho (678-81)
80. St. Leo II (682-83)
81. St. Benedict II (684-85)
82. John V (685-86)
83. Conon (686-87)
84. St. Sergius I (687-701)

85. John VI (701-05)
86. John VII (705-07)
87. Sisinnius (708)
88. Constantine (708-15)
89. St. Gregory II (715-31)
90. St. Gregory III (731-41)
91. St. Zachary (741-52)
92. Stephen II (III) (752-57)
93. St. Paul I (757-67)
94. Stephen III (IV) (767-72)
95. Adrian I (772-95)
96. St. Leo III (795-816)
97. Stephen IV (V) (816-17)
98. St. Paschal I (817-24)
99. Eugene II (824-27)
100. Valentine (827)
101. Gregory IV (827-44)
102. Sergius II (844-47)
103. St. Leo IV (847-55)
104. Benedict III (855-58)
105. St. Nicholas I (the Great) (858-67)
106. Adrian II (867-72)
107. John VIII (872-82)
108. Marinus I (882-84)
109. St. Adrian III (884-85)
110. Stephen V (VI) (885-91)
111. Formosus (891-96)
112. Boniface VI (896)
113. Stephen VI (VII) (896-97)
114. Romanus (897)
115. Theodore II (897)
116. John IX (898-900)
117. Benedict IV (900-03)
118. Leo V (903)
119. Sergius III (904-11)
120. Anastasius III (911-13)
121. Lando (913-14)
122. John X (914-28)
123. Leo VI (928)
124. Stephen VIII (929-31)

125. John XI (931-35)
126. Leo VII (936-39)
127. Stephen IX (939-42)
128. Marinus II (942-46)
129. Agapetus II (946-55)
130. John XII (955-63)
131. Leo VIII (963-64)
132. Benedict V (964)
133. John XIII (965-72)
134. Benedict VI (973-74)
135. Benedict VII (974-83)
136. John XIV (983-84)
137. John XV (985-96)
138. Gregory V (996-99)
139. Sylvester II (999-1003)
140. John XVII (1003)
141. John XVIII (1003-09)
142. Sergius IV (1009-12)
143. Benedict VIII (1012-24)
144. John XIX (1024-32)
145. Benedict IX (1032-45)
146. Sylvester III (1045)
147. Benedict IX (1045)
148. Gregory VI (1045-46)
149. Clement II (1046-47)
150. Benedict IX (1047-48)
151. Damasus II (1048)
152. St. Leo IX (1049-54)
153. Victor II (1055-57)
154. Stephen X (1057-58)
155. Nicholas II (1058-61)
156. Alexander II (1061-73)
157. St. Gregory VII (1073-85)
158. Blessed Victor III (1086-87)
159. Blessed Urban II (1088-99)
160. Paschal II (1099-1118)
161. Gelasius II (1118-19)
162. Callistus II (1119-24)
163. Honorius II (1124-30)
164. Innocent II (1130-43)

165. Celestine II (1143-44)
166. Lucius II (1144-45)
167. Blessed Eugene III (1145-53)
168. Anastasius IV (1153-54)
169. Adrian IV (1154-59)
170. Alexander III (1159-81)
171. Lucius III (1181-85)
172. Urban III (1185-87)
173. Gregory VIII (1187)
174. Clement III (1187-91)
175. Celestine III (1191-98)
176. Innocent III (1198-1216)
177. Honorius III (1216-27)
178. Gregory IX (1227-41)
179. Celestine IV (1241)
180. Innocent IV (1243-54)
181. Alexander IV (1254-61)
182. Urban IV (1261-64)
183. Clement IV (1265-68)
184. Blessed Gregory X (1271-76)
185. Blessed Innocent V (1276)
186. Adrian V (1276)
187. John XXI (1276-77)
188. Nicholas III (1277-80)
189. Martin IV (1281-85)
190. Honorius IV (1285-87)
191. Nicholas IV (1288-92)
192. St. Celestine V (1294)
193. Boniface VIII (1294-1303)
194. Blessed Benedict XI (1303-04)
195. Clement V (1305-14)
196. John XXII (1316-34)
197. Benedict XII (1334-42)
198. Clement VI (1342-52)
199. Innocent VI (1352-62)
200. Blessed Urban V (1362-70)
201. Gregory XI (1370-78)
202. Urban VI (1378-89)
203. Boniface IX (1389-1404)
204. Innocent VII (1404-06)

205. Gregory XII (1406-15)
206. Martin V (1417-31)
207. Eugene IV (1431-47)
208. Nicholas V (1447-55)
209. Callistus III (1455-58)
210. Pius II (1458-64)
211. Paul II (1464-71)
212. Sixtus IV (1471-84)
213. Innocent VIII (1484-92)
214. Alexander VI (1492-1503)
215. Pius III (1503)
216. Julius II (1503-13)
217. Leo X (1513-21)
218. Adrian VI (1522-23)
219. Clement VII (1523-34)
220. Paul III (1534-49)
221. Julius III (1550-55)
222. Marcellus II (1555)
223. Paul IV (1555-59)
224. Pius IV (1559-65)
225. St. Pius V (1566-72)
226. Gregory XIII (1572-85)
227. Sixtus V (1585-90)
228. Urban VII (1590)
229. Gregory XIV (1590-91)
230. Innocent IX (1591)
231. Clement VIII (1592-1605)
232. Leo XI (1605)
233. Paul V (1605-21)
234. Gregory XV (1621-23)
235. Urban VIII (1623-44)
236. Innocent X (1644-55)
237. Alexander VII (1655-67)
238. Clement IX (1667-69)
239. Clement X (1670-76)
240. Blessed Innocent XI (1676-89)
241. Alexander VIII (1689-91)
242. Innocent XII (1691-1700)
243. Clement XI (1700-21)
244. Innocent XIII (1721-24)

245. Benedict XIII (1724-30)
246. Clement XII (1730-40)
247. Benedict XIV (1740-58)
248. Clement XIII (1758-69)
249. Clement XIV (1769-74)
250. Pius VI (1775-99)
251. Pius VII (1800-23)
252. Leo XII (1823-29)
253. Pius VIII (1829-30)
254. Gregory XVI (1831-46)
255. St. Pius IX (1846-78)
256. Leo XIII (1878-1903)
257. St. Pius X (1903-14)
258. Benedict XV (1914-22)
259. Pius XI (1922-39)
260. St. Pius XII (1939-58)
261. St. John XXIII (1958-63)
262. Paul VI (1963-78)
263. John Paul I (1978)
264. St. John Paul II (1978-2005)
265. Benedict XVI (2005-2013)
266. Rutherford I (2011 -)

Roman Empire

Gaius Julius Caesar
Augustus (Imperator Caesar Augustus)
Tiberius (Tiberius Caesar Augustus)
Caligula (Gaius Caesar Augustus Germanicus)
Claudius (Tiberius Claudius Caesar Augustus Germanicus)
Nero (Nero Claudius Caesar Augustus Germanicus)
Galba (Servius Galba Caesar Augustus)
Otho (Marcus Otho Caesar Augustus)
Vitellius (Aulus Vitellius Germanicus Augustus)
Vespasianus (Caesar Vespasianus Augustus)
Titus (Titus Caesar Vespasianus Augustus)
Domitianus (Caesar Domitianus Augustus)
Nerva (Nerva Caesar Augustus)
Trajanus (Caesar Nerva Traianus Augustus)

Hadrianus (Caesar Traianus Hadrianus Augustus)
Antoninus Pius (Titus Aelius Hadrianus Antoninus Augustus Pius)
Marcus Aurelius (Marcus Aurelius Antoninus)
Lucius Verus (Lucius Aurelius Verus)
Commodus (Lucius Aelius Aurelius Commodus)
Pertinax (Publius Helvius Pertinax)
Didius Julianus (Marcus Didius Severus Julianus)
Septimius Severus (Lucius Septimius Severus Pertinax)
Caracalla (Marcus Aurelius Antoninus)
Geta (Publius Septimius Geta)
Macrinus (Marcus Opellius Severus Macrinus)
Diadumenianus (Marcus Opellius Antoninus Diadumenianus)
Elagabalus (Marcus Aurelius Antoninus)
Severus Alexander (Marcus Aurelius Severus Alexander)
Maximinus Thrax (Gaius Julius Verus Maximinus)
Gordianus I (Marcus Antonius Gordianus Sempronianus
    Romanus Africanus)
Gordianus II (Marcus Antonius Gordianus Sempronianus
    Romanus Africanus)
Pupienus (Marcus Clodius Pupienus Maximus)
Balbinus (Decimus Caelius Calvinus Balbinus)
Gordianus III (Marcus Antonius Gordianus)
Philippus (Marcus Julius Philippus)
Philippus II (Marcus Julius Severus Philippus)
Decius (Gaius Messius Quintus Traianus Decius)
Herennius Etruscus (Quintus Herennius Etruscus Messius Decius)
Hostilianus (Gaius Valens Hostilianus Messius Quintus)
Trebonianus Gallus (Gaius Vibius Trebonianus Gallus)
Volusianus (Gaius Vibius Afinius Gallus Veldumnianus
    Volusianus)
Aemilianus (Marcus Aemilius Aemilianus)
Valerianus (Publius Licinius Valerianus)
Gallienus (Publius Licinius Egnatius Gallienus)
Saloninus (Publius Licinius Cornelius Saloninus Valerianus)
Claudius Gothicus (Marcus Aurelius Claudius)
Quintillus (Marcus Aurelius Claudius Quintillus)
Aurelianus (Lucius Domitius Aurelianus)
Tacitus (Marcus Claudius Tacitus)
Florianus (Marcus Annius Florianus)
Probus (Marcus Aurelius Probus)

Carus (Marcus Aurelius Carus)
Carinus (Marcus Aurelius Carinus)
Numerianus (Marcus Aurelius Numerianus)
Diocletianus (Gaius Aurelius Valerius Diocletianus)
Maximianus (Marcus Aurelius Valerius Maximianus)
Galerius (Galerius Valerius Maximianus)
Constantius I (Flavius Valerius Constantius)
Constantinus I (Flavius Valerius Constantinus)
Severus (Flavius Valerius Severus)
Maxentius (Marcus Aurelius Valerius Maxentius)
Licinius (Valerius Licinianus Licinius)
Maximinus Daza (Galerius Valerius Maximinus)
Valerius Valens (Aurelius Valerius Valens)
Martinianus (Sextus Marcius Martinianus)
Constantinus II (Flavius Claudius Constantinus)
Constantius II (Flavius Julius Constantius)
Constans (Flavius Julius Constans)
Vetranio (Flavius Claudius Julianus)
Jovianus (Flavius Jovianus)
Valentinianus I (Valentinianus)
Valens
Gratianus
Valentinianus II
Theodosius I
Magnus Maximus
Victor (Flavius Victor)
Eugenius
Honorius
Constantinus III (Flavius Claudius Constantinus)
Constans II
Constantius III
Joannes
Valentinianus III (Placidus Valentinianus)
Petronius Maximus
Avitus (Eparchius Avitus)
Majorianus (Julius Valerius Maiorianus)
Libius Severus
Anthemius (Procopius Anthemius)
Olybrius (Anicius Olybrius)
Glycerius

Julius Nepos
Romulus Augustus
Papa Sanctus Simplicius
...
etc. *(see continuation therefrom in previous list)*

Made in the USA
Middletown, DE
20 April 2022

64242626R00029